CLIMATE Change

PROBLEMS and PROGRESS

The Danger of Greenhouse Gases

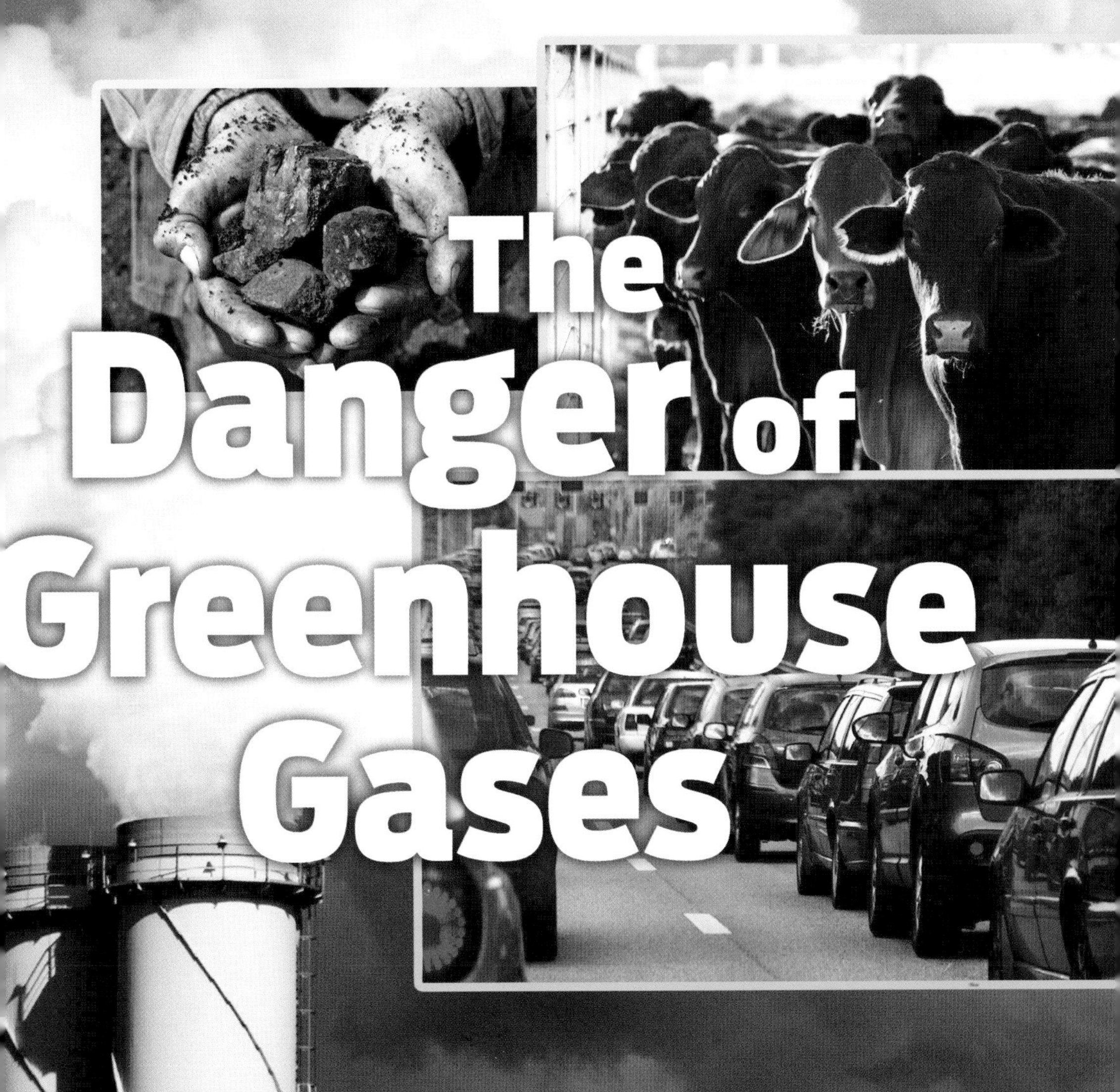

The Danger of Greenhouse Gases

Extreme Weather

The Future of Biodiversity

The Organic Lifestyle

Preserving Energy

Recycling Works!

Renewable Energy in Action

Saving Water

The Vital Role of Deserts and Forests

What Is Climate Change?

The Danger of Greenhouse Gases

James Shoals

Mason Crest

Mason Crest
450 Parkway Drive, Suite D
Broomall, PA 19008
www.masoncrest.com

Printed and bound in the United States of America.

Series ISBN: 978-1-4222-4353-4
Hardback ISBN: 978-1-4222-4354-1
EBook ISBN: 978-1-4222-7449-1

First printing
1 3 5 7 9 8 6 4 2

Cover photographs by Dreamstime: Vyacheslav Svetlichnyy (left); John Casey (right); Alexandragl (bottom). Shutterstock: VanderWolf Images (bkgd.).

Library of Congress Cataloging-in-Publication Data
Names: Shoals, James, author. Title: The danger of greenhouse gases / by James Shoals.
Description: Broomall, PA : Mason Crest, [2019] | Series: Climate challenges: problems and progress | Includes bibliographical references and index.
Identifiers: LCCN 2019013877| ISBN 9781422243534 (series) | ISBN 9781422243541 (hardback) | ISBN 9781422274491 (ebook)
Subjects: LCSH: Greenhouse gases--Environmental aspects--Juvenile literature.
Classification: LCC TD885.5.G73 S534 2019 | DDC 363.738/742--dc23 LC record available at https://lccn.loc.gov/2019013877

QR Codes disclaimer:

CONTENTS

KEY ICONS TO LOOK FOR

Words to Understand: These words with their easy-to-understand definitions will increase the reader's understanding of the text, while building vocabulary skills.

Sidebars: This boxed material within the main text allows readers to build knowledge, gain insights, explore possibilities, and broaden their perspectives by weaving together additional information to provide realistic and holistic perspectives.

Educational Videos: Readers can view videos by scanning our QR codes, providing them with additional educational content to supplement the text. Examples include news coverage, moments in history, speeches, iconic moments, and much more!

Text-Dependent Questions: These questions send the reader back to the text for more careful attention to the evidence presented here.

Research Projects: Readers are pointed toward areas of further inquiry connected to each chapter. Suggestions are provided for projects that encourage deeper research and analysis.

Series Glossary of Key Terms: This back-of-the-book glossary contains terminology used throughout this series. Words found here increase the reader's ability to read and comprehend higher-level books and articles in this field.

WORDS TO UNDERSTAND

accumulation the quantity of something that has increased over a period

aerosol a substance that is kept in a container under high pressure so that it can be sprayed

anthropogenic pollutants generated by human activities

biomass animal dung and other animal waste used as a fuel

compost a mixture made by the decomposition of plant and vegetable waste, to add in soil

deforestation cutting down a large number of trees

ecosystem a community of living organisms and their interaction with each other and their physical environment such as air, soil, and water

eruption to emit or discharge with a force

fermentation the process of breakdown of the food by microorganisms such as yeast

hydroelectric power electricity generated with the power of flowing water

Industrial Revolution a period of development in industries, agriculture, textile, and transportation

infrared a type of light that can be felt as heat but cannot be seen

magnitude of great extent, importance

permafrost a subsurface layer of soil that remains frozen throughout the year, usually in the polar regions

pesticide a substance that is used to kill those insects that damage crops

photochemical a chemical reaction caused by light

precipitation water released from clouds as rain, snow, hail, or sleet

radiate to emit energy in the form of rays, heat, and waves

reservoir a large quantity of something that can be used anytime

sedative a medicinal drug that makes one fall asleep

semiconductor a solid substance that allows electricity to pass through it when its temperature increases

smog a mixture of smoke and fog in the atmosphere

solvent a substance which is capable of dissolving a solid substance

stratosphere a part of Earth's atmosphere that is 10–50 km above the surface

sublimation the process in which a solid substance changes into gas or vice versa without becoming liquid

topography the physical features of the earth such as hills, mountains, rivers, etc.

transpiration the process in which water from leaves passes into the atmosphere as water vapor

volatile any liquid or substance that can quickly change into gas

wetland an area of land fully or partially submerged in water

INTRODUCTION

The Earth is wrapped in a blanket of atmosphere, made up of many gases. Some of these gases, known as the greenhouse gases (GHGs), have the ability to trap and store the heat **radiated** by the Earth. The Earth's atmosphere is kept slightly warmer due to the greenhouse effect. This natural phenomenon enables the existence of life on Earth. However, human activities are gradually destroying the delicate balance of nature by releasing an excess of GHGs into the atmosphere. This has harmful effects on the global climate and **topography**.

As global warming increases, its effects are felt worldwide. Sea levels are rising and now the Earth is covered with a warmer atmospheric layer near the ground. GHGs such as carbon dioxide (CO_2), methane, and nitrous oxide are added to the atmosphere due to daily human activities. There is a great need for individuals and businesses to reduce their carbon footprint to prevent global warming.

Greenhouse Effect

An increase in the concentration of GHGs also increases the **magnitude** of the greenhouse effect. This leads to a rise in the temperature of the Earth's surface. This rise in temperatures is causing global warming, which in turn accounts for major climatic changes in our planet.

Heating the Atmosphere

About 31 percent of the solar radiation is reflected back into space, while the Earth's atmosphere absorbs 69 percent of it. The surface of the Earth is heated by sunlight that passes through the atmosphere. Upon heating, the Earth's surface emits infrared rays that warm the air above it. The GHGs present in the Earth's atmosphere absorb and reemit this infrared radiation. Thus, they act like the glass in a greenhouse, which prevents the heat from escaping.

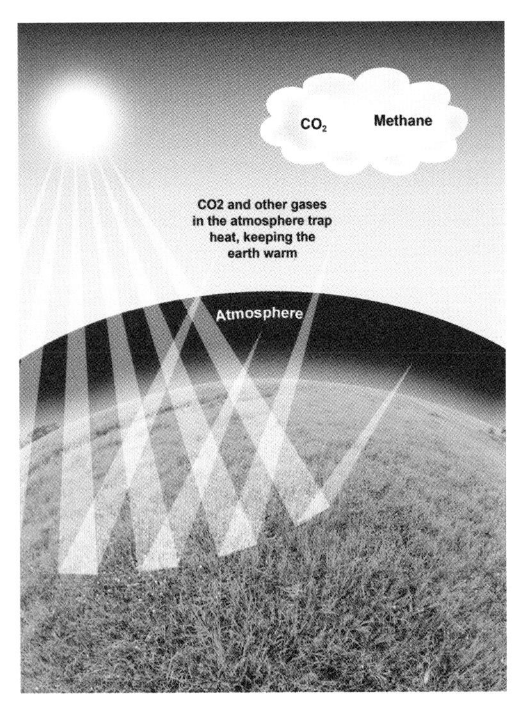

CO2
Methane
CO2 and other gases in the atmosphere trap heat, keeping the earth warm
Atmosphere

Human Contribution

Human activities, such as excess burning of fossil fuels, release additional GHGs into the atmosphere, thus increasing the greenhouse effect. CO_2, methane, and nitrous oxide are the main gases that contribute to the GH effect. There are other gases as well that add to the GH effect. However, only a small percentage of them exist in the atmosphere.

Climate Facts

- Among all the GHGs, CO_2 has the highest concentrations in the atmosphere.
- The concentration of CO_2 was less during the glacial periods. Such periods were marked by colder temperatures.

Greenhouse Gases

The GHGs present in our atmosphere have supported the existence of life on Earth. These gases trap solar heat within the Earth's atmosphere and allow its temperature to be warmer and more stable. The most common GHGs are methane, CO_2, nitrogen oxides (NOx), and fluorinated gases (F-gases). GHGs act like a blanket and keep the Earth's temperature thirty degrees warmer than it would be otherwise.

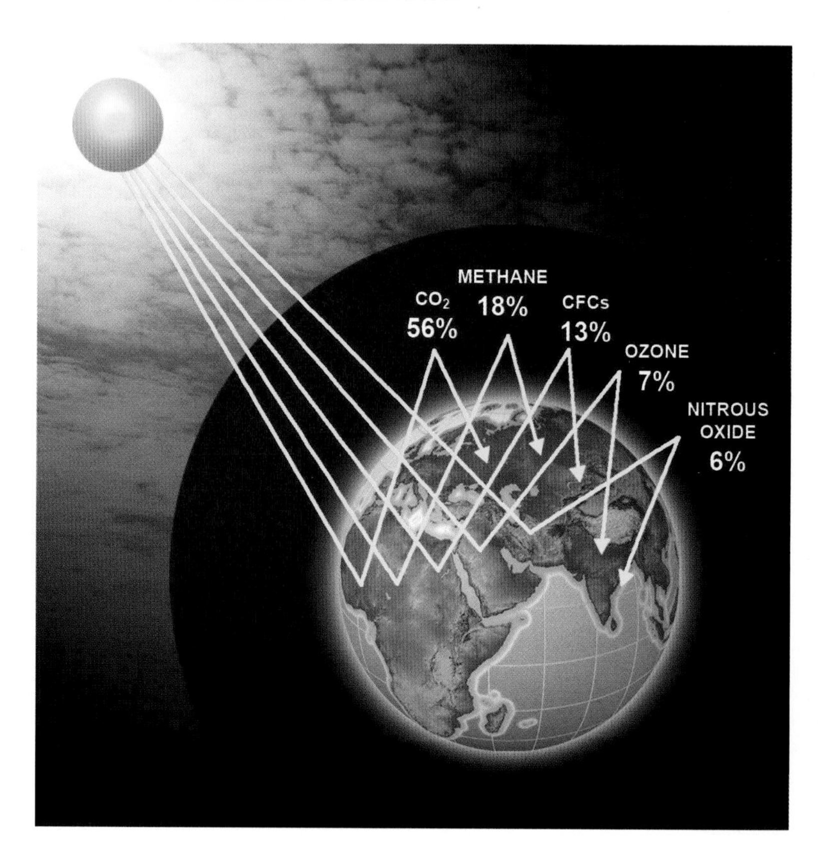

Constitution

GHGs constitute only 1 percent of the total atmosphere. The rest of the atmosphere comprises oxygen and nitrogen. Some of the GHGs occur naturally within the atmosphere such as water vapor, while the others such as chlorofluorocarbons are released due to human activities. Different GHGs have different durations in the atmosphere and different warming capabilities.

How do GHGs work?

GHGs allow sunlight to enter the atmosphere freely. When sunlight reaches the Earth's surface, some of it is reflected back towards space as **infrared** radiation. GHGs absorb this infrared radiation and trap its heat within the atmosphere. Each GHG molecule is made up of three or more atoms that are loosely bonded together. These molecules are able to absorb the heat within them, which makes them vibrate. They eventually release this heat energy, which is further absorbed by another molecule. In this way, the heat is trapped and transferred by GHGs.

Global Warming Potential (GWP)

GWP refers to a measure that estimates how much a gas contributes to global warming as compared to CO_2. The ratio of heat trapped by one unit mass of the GHG to that of one unit mass of CO_2 determines the GWP of a GHG.

Climate Facts

- Just over two pounds (1 kg) of CO_2 would fill a large family fridge. One ton of CO_2 would fill a large home.

- Without the greenhouse effect, the average temperature would be about -2°F (-18°C) rather than the current 57°F (14°C).

Methane

Methane (CH_4) is an odorless and colorless gas that contributes greatly to the greenhouse effect. It is the simplest hydrocarbon and is highly combustible. Since the time of the industrialization boom, the concentration of methane in the atmosphere has increased many times over. Methane is responsible for almost half of the planet's human-induced warming.

Uses

Methane has a GWP of 21, which means that it is twenty-one times more effective than CO_2 in trapping heat. If methane is released directly into the atmosphere, it causes global warming. To avoid environmental problems, methane is used as a fuel to generate energy. It forms a major component of the natural gas found beneath the surface of the Earth.

Sources

Methane is generated naturally by the decomposition of organic wastes in the absence of oxygen. **Wetlands**, rice paddies, termites, oceans, permafrost, and wildfires generate large amounts of methane. Human-influenced sources such as landfills, natural gas leaks, agricultural activities, fossil fuel mining, wastewater treatment, and certain industrial processes generate 75 percent of the methane emissions worldwide.

Methane Sink

A methane molecule remains in the atmosphere for approximately nine to fifteen years, after which hydroxyl radicals oxidize it into CO_2 and water. Certain microbes present in well-drained soils rely on methane for carbon and energy. They constitute approximately 5 percent of the total methane sink from the atmosphere.

However, due to the warming of the Arctic, the methane buried under the Arctic seafloor may escape and speed up global warming.

Cattle

Cattle, sheep, buffalo, and goats are ruminant animals—animals with four stomachs and a unique digestive system. They graze on plant matter and release methane through their digestion process. A cow produces 175-240 pounds (80–110 kg) of methane in a year. In the US, about one hundred million cattle discharge about 5.5 million metric tons of methane per year. Globally, ruminant animals release about eighty million metric tons of methane per year.

Climate Facts

- Methane levels may rise significantly in the future if global warming melts the frozen ground in the Arctic.
- Trace amounts of sulfur compounds are added to commercial methane to detect leakage and avoid explosions.

Carbon Dioxide

CO_2 is an atmospheric gas whose one molecule consists of one carbon atom and two oxygen atoms. It is produced by burning carbon compounds and by respiration. CO_2 is a GHG and contributes significantly to global warming. Once emitted, it can remain in the atmosphere for up to a hundred years.

Increase in CO_2

CO_2 in the atmosphere has increased by about 30 percent since the early 1800s. Human activities such as the burning of fossil fuels and **deforestation** have contributed to the increase of CO_2 in the air. The combustion of organic matter in the presence of oxygen is directly responsible for producing CO_2.

Human Activities

From the Industrial Revolution until 2018, the atmospheric concentrations of CO_2 have risen to nearly 40 percent. The use of fossil fuels such as coal, oil, petroleum, and gas in vehicles, power plants, and industries releases large amounts of CO_2. Deforestation prevents the **accumulation** of carbon in plants. Energy efficiency as well as reduction in the consumption of energy is required to avoid climate change.

Natural Sources and Sinks

All animals and humans in the process of respiration breathe out CO_2. Plants take in CO_2 for their nutrition and growth and release oxygen in return. Various microorganisms produce CO_2 through the process of **fermentation**. Volcanic eruptions and hot springs also release CO_2. Oceans act as a large carbon sink and absorb large amounts of CO_2 from the sea surfaces.

NASA data on CO_2

Climate Facts

- Every single day, seventy million tons of CO_2 are released into the atmosphere.
- CO_2 in its dry form is known as dry ice.

Water Vapor

Water vapor is the gaseous form of the water present in our atmosphere. It is the most abundant and the most important GHG. Water is converted into water vapor through evaporation, **sublimation**, and **transpiration**. Clouds, fog, and haze are all forms of water vapor.

Sources and Sinks

Water vapor has a very short atmospheric lifetime. It is continuously added to the atmosphere through evaporation and removed through condensation in the form of rain and snow. Atmospheric water vapor is highly reactive and difficult to measure due to the changing weather conditions. Its concentrations change from one place to another. Higher temperature means more water vapor.

Vicious Circle

Water vapor contributes to around 95 percent of global warming. As the average temperature of the Earth increases, so does the average evaporation. Warmer air is able to hold more moisture. A higher concentration of water vapor in the atmosphere is able to absorb more heat. Thus, the rise in water vapor further contributes to the greenhouse effect and global warming, making it a vicious circle.

Clouds

More water vapor in the atmosphere due to global warming also means that there is a rise in the formation of clouds in the sky. More clouds trap more heat within the atmosphere. However, clouds also have a moderating effect on climate as they help reflect a portion of solar radiation. Low, thick clouds reflect the radiation and cool the surface of Earth, while high, thin clouds trap heat and warm the surface of the Earth.

Climate Facts

- **During the 1990s, one-third of the rise in global temperatures was due to an increase of water vapor in the atmosphere.**

- **Boiling water produces steam, which comprises up to 70 percent of the total greenhouse effect.**

Nitrous Oxide

Nitrous oxide (N_2O) is a colorless greenhouse gas with a sweet odor. This greenhouse gas has a high GWP (310), a long lifetime, and the ability to destroy ozone. N_2O is also known as "laughing gas" since it creates tingling sensations and feelings of euphoria upon consumption. For this reason, it is also used as a **sedative** in the medical industry.

Denitrification

N_2O is produced naturally through the breakdown of nitrogen by the bacteria in soils and oceans. This process is known as denitrification. It produces N_2O as a by-product. Nutrient-rich discharges in the world's oceans such as agriculture runoff and sewage have resulted in large-scale denitrification in open water. Over 60 percent of N_2O is produced due to these biological processes.

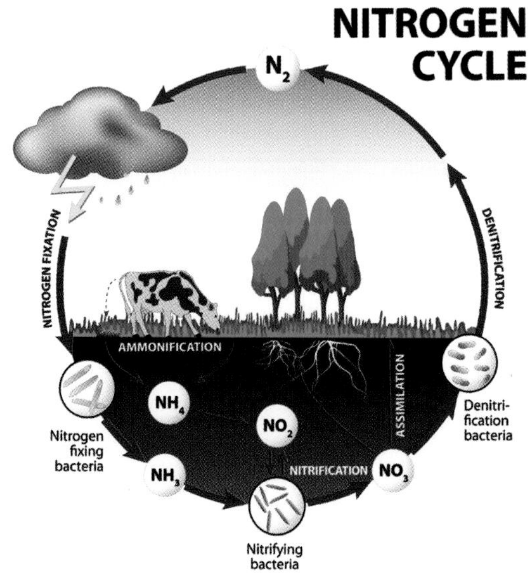

Nitrogen cycle explained

Man-made Sources

Human-influenced sources of N_2O include animal manure management and the increasing use of fertilizers in agriculture. Industrial processes such as combustion in fossil fuel-fired power plants, nylon production, nitric acid production, and vehicle emissions also contribute to a rise in N_2O. Its concentrations have increased since the beginning of **Industrial Revolution**.

Sinks

The majority of atmospheric N_2O is removed from the **stratosphere** by reaction with light and excited oxygen atoms. The breakup of N_2O molecules in this way is known as photolysis. A very small amount of N_2O is also converted into nitrogen gas by the bacteria present in soil.

Climate Facts

- N_2O concentrations in the atmosphere have increased up to 16 percent between 1750 and 1998.

- Globally, oceans are believed to add around three million tons of nitrous oxide to the atmosphere each year.

Other GHGs

Apart from the five major GHGs present in the atmosphere, some other GHGs are present in trace quantities. Such gases include numerous fluorinated gases and halocarbons. Their lifetime ranges from a few months to more than four thousand years, with GWPs up to ten thousand times that of CO_2. They are produced for use in a variety of industrial processes.

Hydrofluorocarbons (HFCs)

HFCs are compounds consisting of hydrogen, fluorine, and carbon. These chemicals were used as a replacement for chlorofluorocarbons in refrigeration and air conditioning, which cause ozone depletion. They have long atmospheric lifetimes, ranging from 14 years to 260 years, and have strong global warming potential. HFCs need to be phased out from the atmosphere and the existing refrigerants need to be disposed of properly in order to deal with the global warming issue.

Chlorofluorocarbons

Chlorofluorocarbons are a group of compounds that consist of carbon, chlorine, and fluorine. They are toxic compounds with a faintly sweet odor. They were used in **aerosol** applications as refrigerants and **solvents**. Although their use has now been banned, they will continue to add to the greenhouse effect due to their long atmospheric lifetimes.

Black Carbon

Though black carbon, or soot, is not a greenhouse gas, it is second only to CO_2 in trapping atmospheric heat. It is made of many tiny particles, which mix with dust, sulfates, and other materials that rise from the ground. Rising through the atmosphere, it reaches the clouds and mixes with water droplets. **Precipitation** again brings the black carbon back to earth. When it falls on ice and snow, it darkens their reflective surfaces and does not allow enough sunlight to bounce back out to space. This adds to global warming.

The soot rising from chimneys, hut stoves, forest fires, diesel-fueled trucks, ocean liners, brick kilns, and gas flares plays a significant role in accelerating global warming.

Climate Facts

- According to the National Oceanic and Atmospheric Administration (NOAA), the demand for HFCs is expected to increase globally.

- HCFCs and CFCs are together known as halocarbons.

Some other GHGs that have certain extreme effects are fluorocarbons, sulfur hexafluoride, and nitrogen trifluoride. Though these gases are present in small quantities, they contribute to global warming. These gases can stay in the atmosphere for hundreds or thousands of years.

Perfluorocarbons

Fluorocarbons or perfluorocarbons are strong GHGs made up of strong carbon and fluorine bonds. They have atmospheric lifetimes of more than a thousand years. They are man-made chemicals composed of fluorine and carbon. They are mostly nonreactive odorless and colorless gases. These gases are used in various medical applications, in cosmetics, and in manufacturing **semiconductors**.

Sulfur Hexafluoride (SF_6)

Sulfur hexafluoride (SF_6) is a colorless, odorless, nontoxic, nonflammable, man-made gas. Sulfur hexafluoride is believed to be the most potent GHG with a GWP of over a one hundred-year period. There has been a 7 percent increase in SF_6 during the 1980s and 1990s. It has an atmospheric lifetime of up to three thousand two hundred years. It is mostly used in magnesium-producing industries.

Nitrogen Trifluoride (NF_3)

Nitrogen trifluoride (NF_3) is a synthetic, colorless, stable, and toxic gas. It has a moldy odor, and is used in the manufacturing of flat-screen TV sets, computer screens, cell phones, etc. It has a GWP of 17,200 over a one hundred-year time scale. It has an atmospheric lifetime of 740 years. According to a team of researchers, the concentration of NF_3 is four times more than what was expected.

Climate Facts

- A hybrid GHG derived from PFCs (Perfluorinated Chemicals) and SF6 is the most powerful greenhouse gas yet discovered.

- Trace GHGs are also referred to as High Global Warming Potential gases ("High GWP Gases").

Indirect GHGs

Some indirect GHGs do not directly trap heat but contribute to the GH effect. Once they are released into the atmosphere, they form substances that enhance the greenhouse effect. Indirect **anthropogenic** GHGs are carbon monoxide (CO), hydrogen gas, non-methane **volatile** organic compounds, ammonia, and sulfur dioxide.

Carbon Monoxide (CO)

Carbon monoxide (CO) is a toxic gas produced due to the impartial burning of fossil fuels. It increases the global warming potential of GHGs by destroying the hydroxyl (OH) radicals in the air. These OH radicals are useful for the breakdown of GHGs such as carbon dioxide and methane. Carbon monoxide also helps in the formation of tropospheric ozone and carbon dioxide, which are major greenhouse gases. It is a short-lived gas and mostly occurs in densely populated regions. Automobiles and charcoal burning emit high levels of carbon monoxide.

Hydrogen Gas

Hydrogen gas is used as a fuel and has the potential to replace fossil fuels in the future. The leakage of hydrogen gas from cars, hydrogen production sites and processes, and by transportation is unavoidable. If hydrogen replaces fossil fuels completely, 60–120 trillion grams of hydrogen would be discharged into the atmosphere each year. The production of hydrogen gas by using natural gas and burning fossil fuels also releases carbon dioxide.

Volatile Organic Compounds

Volatile organic compounds (VOCs) are a group of weak indirect GHGs that help in the formation of tropospheric ozone in the atmosphere. VOCs include non methane hydrocarbons, alcohols, aldehydes, and organic acids. They are mainly produced by natural sources such as plants and oceans. They are also released by the evaporation of petrol and diesel and by incomplete burning of biomass.

Climate Facts

- Hydrogen gas is lighter than air.
- Carbon monoxide is also known as carbonous oxide.

GHGs and Global Warming

Since 1920, the surface temperature of Earth has increased by 1.4°F (0.8°C). However, the current warming is taking place at a much faster rate. CO_2 emissions from fossil fuel combustion increased by 21.8 percent between 1990 and 2007, while methane and nitrous oxide emissions decreased marginally. The increasing concentration of CO_2 has led to major climate changes.

Plant and Animal Life

Global warming has also had serious effects on plant and animal life. Flowers are blooming earlier and animals are breeding earlier than their natural time. Many animals and plants are becoming extinct due to habitat loss, scarcity of food, and rising temperatures. Various **ecosystems** are destroyed, such as the Arctic region. Food chains have also been disturbed due to climate and temperature changes.

Weather Changes

Global warming is causing an increase in floods, storms, and droughts. High rates of evaporation due to increased temperatures causes higher rainfall. Global warming is causing polar ice caps to melt. This melting may raise the sea level and cause the submergence of coastal and low-lying regions.

Agriculture and Forests

Warmer temperatures and GHG emissions are affecting agriculture too. Irregular rainfall is one of the main reasons for the failure of crops. Some agricultural lands have become too dry for farming. With the rise in global temperatures, several disease-causing microorganisms and pests are on the rise. This has led to widespread diseases in crops, thus reducing overall productivity.

Climate Facts

- The sharpest rise in global temperatures occurred between 1975 and 2010.

- Some butterflies, foxes, and Alpine plants have moved to cooler, higher regions due to global warming.

Ozone Layer

Ozone is a gas made up of three oxygen atoms. It is blue in color and has a strong odor. A wide layer of ozone is found in our stratosphere, extending from fifteen to thirty kilometers above the Earth's surface. It is formed when oxygen atoms react with ultraviolet (UV) radiation.

Ozone Concentration

The thickness of the ozone layer varies depending on latitude, sunspots, and seasons. The total mass of ozone in the atmosphere is about three billion metric tons, but it is only 0.00006 percent of the atmosphere. The peak concentration of ozone occurs at an altitude of roughly thirty-two kilometers above the Earth's surface.

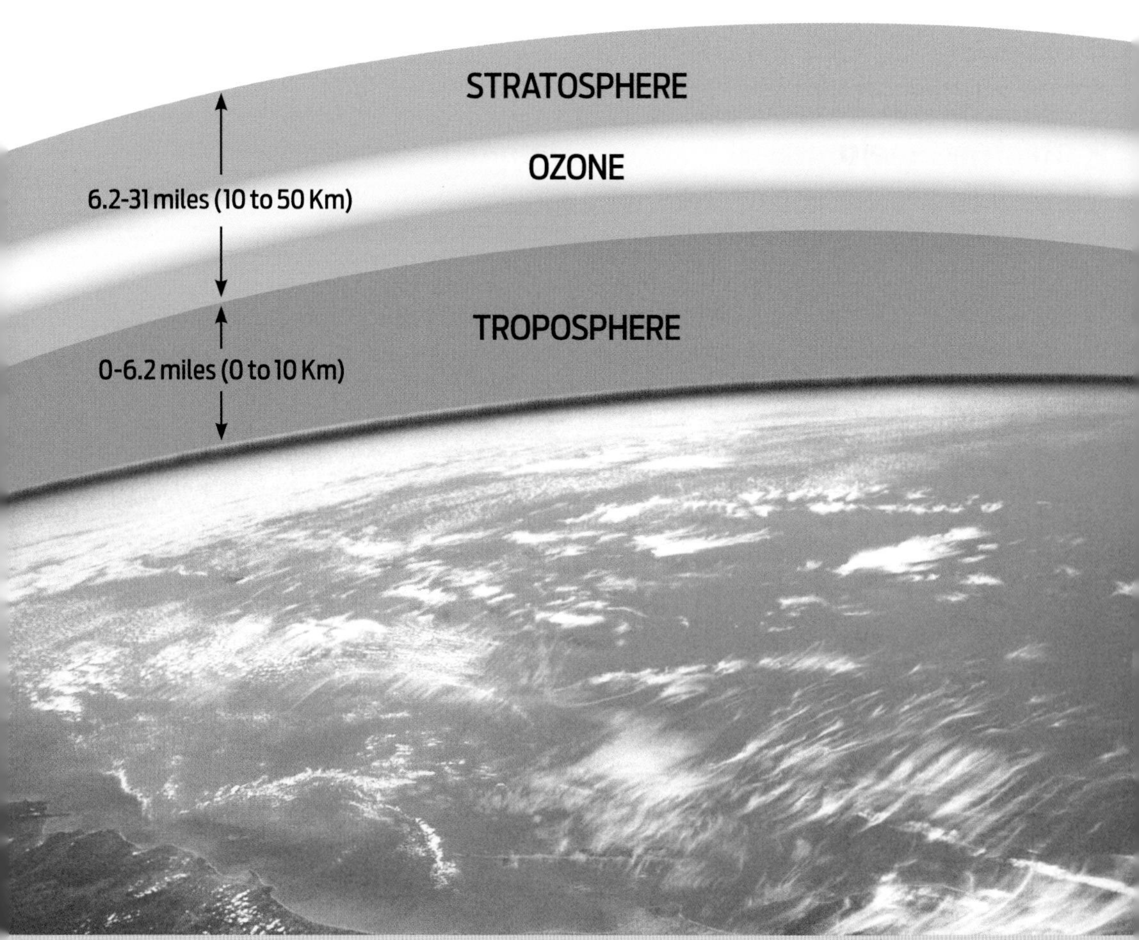

Protective Shield

The ozone layer protects life on Earth by preventing harmful UV rays from reaching the Earth's surface. It is also known as Earth's sunscreen. It absorbs 97–99 percent of high-frequency UV radiation, which may cause diseases such as skin cancer and cataracts. Increased UV radiation can also lead to reduced crop yield, disruptions in the marine food chain, and other environmental problems.

Damage

Over the past sixty years, human activity has harmed this protective layer through chemicals and pollution. Various pollutants and man-made chemicals have damaged the ozone layer. A reduction in the concentration of ozone in the stratosphere is known as the ozone hole.

Climate Facts

- **French physicists, Charles Fabry and Henri Buisson, discovered the ozone layer in 1913.**

- **Scientists estimate that one chlorine atom can destroy one hundred thousand "good" ozone molecules.**

Tropospheric Ozone

Ozone is present in both the upper atmosphere as well as near the ground (the troposphere). The ozone layer in the stratosphere protects life on Earth. However, the ozone that we inhale is a pollutant that causes many health and environmental problems. It also acts as a GHG, which contributes to global warming.

Sources and Sinks

Tropospheric ozone is produced in the troposphere by oxidation or breakdown of volatile organic compounds in solvents such as paints and hair sprays. Pollution from automobiles and industries, and the burning of fossil fuels lead to a greater concentration of carbon and nitrogen molecules in the lower atmosphere. These molecules produce ozone upon reacting with sunlight. Ozone is mainly removed from the atmosphere through **photochemical** breakdown in sunlight.

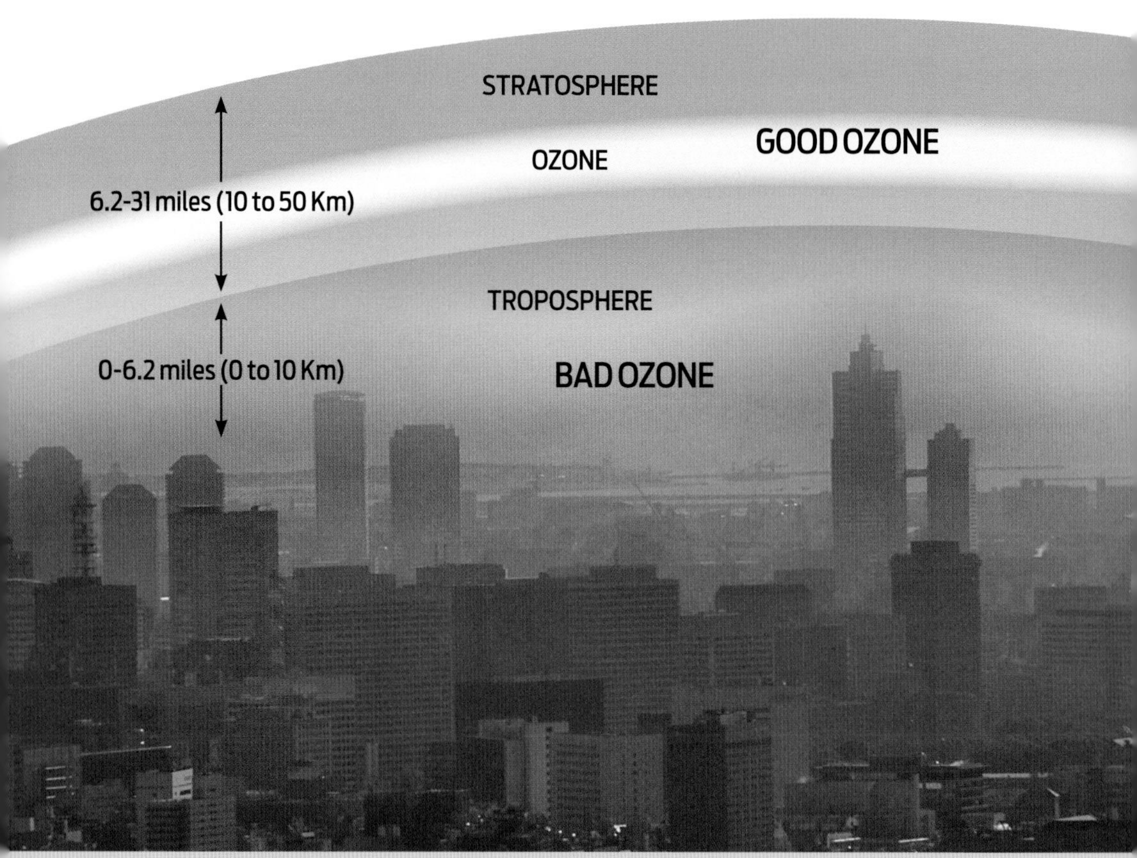

Dangers

Tropospheric ozone poses a great health hazard to human beings, animals, plants, crops, and the environment, and causes harm to various natural and man-made materials. It can cause headaches, respiratory illness, and irritation to the eyes, nose, and throat. People suffering from asthma and other respiratory diseases are at a greater health risk. Tropospheric ozone also destroys crops, trees, and other vegetation. It is a major constituent of photochemical **smog** in cities.

GWP of Ozone

Ozone is three thousand times stronger than CO_2 as a GHG. Since the industrial revolution, the concentrations of ozone in the atmosphere have increased by around 30 percent. It is considered the third most important GHG after CO_2 and methane. Another threat associated with ozone is that it also interacts with, and is affected by, concentrations of methane.

NASA explains ozone depletion

Climate Facts

- Most commercial airline traffic occurs in the lower part of the stratosphere.

- It was in the 1970s that scientists discovered that certain man-made chemicals were capable of destroying the ozone layer of the atmosphere.

Ozone Depletion

As the CFCs and HFCs reach the stratosphere, the UV rays of the sun break them apart and release chlorine atoms that react with ozone. This triggers chemical cycles of ozone destruction. One chlorine atom is capable of breaking apart over one hundred thousand ozone molecules. Such ozone depleting substances (ODSs) stay in the atmosphere for a very long time. Other ODSs are **pesticides**, such as methyl bromide, and halons used in fire extinguishers.

Antarctic Hole

Since more ozone is destroyed than is created naturally, it results in the thinning of the ozone layer all over the planet. Every spring, a hole as large as the United States develops over Antarctica. This is known as the Antarctic ozone hole. The Antarctic ozone hole reached a record size in 2000, when it covered nearly 11.5 million sq. miles (30 million sq. km), roughly the size of the North American continent.

Arctic Hole

Smaller ozone holes also develop every year over the Arctic, in the North Pole. These holes allow harmful UV light to reach the populated areas of Europe. Ozone levels over the northern hemisphere have been dropping by 4 percent per decade. Scientists have predicted that the ozone layer will be restored in the stratosphere by 2065.

Threatened Plants and Animals

Harmful UV rays can pass through water and are threatening aquatic organisms. Plankton, tiny living organisms, are dying because of UV rays. They are a major source of food for a variety of sea organisms, including whales, fish, snail, shrimp, sea stars, and so on. Therefore, if the population of plankton decreases, many marine living organisms will reach the verge of extinction. UV rays also affect the growth of both aquatic and land plants on which life depends.

Climate Facts

- In 1987, the United States and a few other countries signed the Montreal Protocol treaty to phase out the production and use of ozone-depleting substances.

- Every spring for the past twenty years, Punta Arenas, Chile, the southernmost city in the world, has regularly seen high levels of UV-B radiation.

Kyoto Protocol

An international agreement, the Kyoto Protocol, was signed to deal with global warming. The Kyoto Protocol was aimed at fighting the effects of human activities on natural climate. It was adopted at Kyoto, Japan, in December 1997 to control the GHGs. More than 190 countries have signed and ratified it.

Targets

Under the protocol, each country agreed to reach a target relating to national reduction in greenhouse emissions. The combined effort of all countries was expected to cut down the total GHG emissions by at least 5 percent by 2008-2012. The aim of the treaty was to reduce the overall emissions of the six main GHGs—carbon dioxide, methane, nitrous oxide, sulfur hexafluoride, HFCs, and PFCs.

Projects

Various initiatives and programs were introduced to reduce the GHG emissions. Many countries, such as Italy, switched to renewable sources of energy and curbed the use of fossil fuels. Various companies and businesses have undertaken projects such as tree planting, creating wind farms, and solar energy.

United States and Kyoto Protocol

The United States is responsible for approximately one-fourth of the world's greenhouse gas emissions. The US initially withdrew its support to the Kyoto Protocol as it felt that the economic costs were too high as compared to the benefits. It eventually signed but did not ratify the protocol, which means that it accepts the standards of the Kyoto Protocol but does not find it necessary to adhere to it.

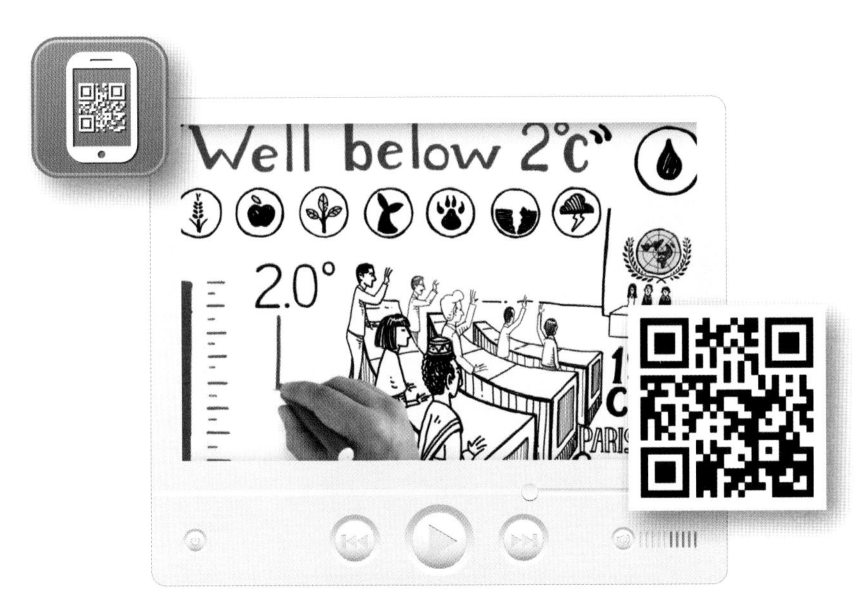

Next step: The Paris Accord

Climate Facts

- National targets ranged from 8 percent reductions for the European Union and some others, to 6 percent for Japan.

- Some countries with low emissions, such as Iceland, were permitted by the Kyoto Protocol to increase them.

Food Waste

Food waste is also responsible for the emission of GHGs. Wasted food is sent to landfills, where it rots and emits methane. Some foods have more effect on the atmosphere than do others. Research shows that the milk wasted each year in Britain accounts for the emission of one hundred thousand tons of CO_2 into the atmosphere.

Waste Food Emissions

Every year nearly one-third, or 1.43 billion tons, of the food produced for human consumption all over the world is wasted. The United Kingdom wastes seven million tons of food each year, which costs the nation $10 billion. In the United States, around 40 percent of all edible food is wasted. More than 135 million tons of GHGs are emitted every year due to food wastage, which is 1.5 percent of all emissions.

Sources

Mishandling or improper storage of food during transportation might lead to food waste. Poor training of food handlers contributes to food waste in restaurants. In households, much of the food waste happens due to food spoilage and overpurchasing. Citrus fruits, cherries, sweet potatoes, green vegetables, and onions are the most commonly wasted vegetables.

Reduce Food Waste

People should buy only those food items that they need. They should avoid leftovers. If there are leftovers, freeze them so that they can be eaten later. Food waste can also be turned into **compost** for use in household plants and in gardens.

Climate Facts

- The food sector accounts for around one-third of the global methane emissions and one-fifth of the global CO_2 emissions.
- The amount of milk wasted annually is 92.4 million gallons (350 million l).

The Paris Agreement

While the Kyoto Protocol focused on the impact of CFCs on the atmosphere, the 2015 meetings in Paris had larger ambitions. The gathering brought together nearly 200 nations in an effort to create an agreement to prevent the Earth's climate from increasing.

The Process

After many weeks of debate, the nations assembled in Paris created the Paris Agreement. Under this plan, the 195 nations at the conference would work toward changing how their nations affected global warming, with the goal of keeping the temperature rise of the Earth by 2100 to less than two degrees Celsius (that's about 3.6 degrees Farenheit). Each nation would create a specific plan to reach a set of targets. They would report back every five years starting in 2020. The key to the entire process was the near-universal acceptance of the plan. At first, the United State and China, by far the world's largest producers of greenhouse gases and industrial-based CO_2 and other products, agreed to the plan. "Under the accord, the United States had pledged to cut its greenhouse gas emissions 26 to 28 percent below 2005 levels by 2025 and commit up to $3 billion in aid for poorer countries by 2020," wrote *The New York Times* in 2017.

A Step Back

In 2017, however, President Donald Trump announced that he was taking the United States out of the Paris Agreement. This was a shocking development and one opposed by the majority of Americans and certainly by the world enviromental movement. He said that he was doing so because he felt the agreement put a burden on Americans as the country moved to make changes to reach the targets. He also put more faith in climate-change deniers than his predecessor, President Barack Obama, who fully supported the Paris plan.

The Plan Continues

Many nations around the world continue to work toward the targets set in Paris. Increasing the use of renewable energy, such as solar power, and cutting the use of fossil fuels is a huge first step. The plan remains a strong way to achieve real improvement in the growing climate change crisis. The loss of American leadership, however, was a huge blow. To make things worse, in the years after the accord, additional science and reporting has made it more clear than ever that the problem is not going away and might in fact be getting worse. The need for America and China and other large nations to make significant changes to their countries' lifestyles continues to be vital.

Climate Facts

- In the Paris Agreement, China agreed to level off growth in emissions by 2030.
- A secondary goal of the Paris Accord is to prevent a rise of more than 1.5°C, as well.

Carbon Capture and Storage

Carbon capture and storage is a technology that captures CO_2 from fossil fuel power stations. The captured CO_2 is transported through pipelines to deep underground structures offshore, such as depleted oil and gas **reservoirs** and deep saline aquifers, where it is stored safely. The safe storage of CO_2 helps to tackle global warming and climate change.

Carbon Sources

Carbon is added to the atmosphere through the following:

- the respiration of animals
- the decomposition of organic matter
- the combustion of **biomass**
- industrial processes
- volcanic **eruptions**
- releases from **permafrost**
- mining activities
- forest fires.

Carbon capture and storage in Australia

Carbon Sinks

Carbon is stored inside the Earth in four major reservoirs. It is important to maintain carbon in these reservoirs, so that it does not contribute to global warming.

Oceans: Carbon exists in oceans in the form of dissolved CO_2 as well as in marine organisms. Carbon is also stored in the shells of living organisms.

Living organisms: Plants take in CO_2 and give out oxygen. They use carbon to prepare their food, which is transferred to other living organisms through the food chain.

Sediments: Carbon is also stored in rocks and soil such as limestone. Fossil fuels such as coal, gas, and oil also contain carbon.

Atmosphere: Carbon exists in the atmosphere in the form of GHGs, such as CO_2, CH_4, CO, and chlorofluorocarbons.

Climate Facts

- By burning fossil fuels, we release stored carbon into the atmosphere.
- Planting trees helps in storing the atmospheric carbon.

Carbon Footprint

Carbon footprint refers to the total amount of GHGs produced by an individual, business, or product. The per capita carbon footprint is the highest in the United States. Individuals and organizations can participate in preventing global climate change by taking various steps to reduce their carbon footprint.

Carbon Offsets

Carbon offset is any activity that compensates for the emission of CO_2 and other GHGs into the atmosphere. Examples of carbon-offset projects are energy efficiency improvements, such as installing energy-efficient light bulbs in homes and even work areas.

Alternative Energy

Carbon footprint can be reduced by making use of alternative energy such as wind energy, **hydroelectric power** and solar energy. Such energy sources do not involve any carbon emissions. Purchasing energy-efficient and reusable goods also ensures lesser emission of carbon dioxide and methane. Fuels that are more efficient are replacing fossil fuels.

Consumption

One of the major causes of global warming is the burning of fossil fuels for energy. Everyone can help reduce global warming by using less energy. All the things that use electricity such as lights, computers, and washing machines should be switched off while not in use to avoid wasting energy. Automobiles and other vehicles create a lot of pollution. Car pools and public transportation can help in reducing one's carbon footprint.

Climate Facts

- GHGs are much more effective higher up in the atmosphere, where it is colder, as compared to when near the warm surface of the Earth.

- Transportation in the United States accounts for 33 percent of GHG emissions.

TEXT-DEPENDENT QUESTIONS

1. What are greenhouse gases?
2. What are two sources of methane in the atmosphere?
3. What is another name for nitrous oxide?
4. What era in history began the majority of the increase in greenhouse gases?
5. What is GWP and what does it measure?
6. Name one of the layers of Earth's atmosphere.
7. About how much milk is wasted each year, according to the text?
8. In what year was the Paris Accord on Climate Change signed?

RESEARCH PROJECTS

1. Cows are a big source of methane gas. Some farmers are looking for ways to reduce their animals' output of methane. Research these ways and then make a list to share with a group. Are there farms near you? Visit one and find out how farmers are changing what they feed cows to help with the methane problem.

2. Read about the controversy created when President Donald Trump pulled the United States out of the Paris Climate Accord. What reasons did he give for this? Do you agree with those reasons? Research evidence to back up your opinion of the decision. Discuss with your friends.

3. What is your carbon footprint? Go online and find a carbon footprint calculator and enter the data. What result do you get? How can you modify your lifestyle to reduce your carbon footprint? What are some ways your family could help, too?

FIND OUT MORE

Books

Collins, Anne. *The Climate Change Crisis (Hot Topics).* Minneapolis, MN: Lucent Books, 2018.

Sedjo, Roger. *Surviving Global Warming: Why Eliminating Greenhouse Gases Isn't Enough.* New York: Prometheus Books, 2019.

Swanson, Kristin. *Geoengineering Earth's Climate: Resetting the Thermostat.* New York: Twenty-First Century Books, 2018.

On the Internet

NOAA info on greenhouse gases
ncdc.noaa.gov/monitoring-references/faq/greenhouse-gases.php

National Geographic: Greenhouse Gases
www.nationalgeographic.com/environment/global-warming/greenhouse-gases/

UN News on greenhouse gases
news.un.org/en/story/2018/11/1026391

SERIES GLOSSARY OF KEY TERMS

bioaccumulation the process of the buildup of toxic chemical substances in the body

biodiversity the diversity of plant and animal life in a habitat (or in the world as a whole)

ecosystem refers to a community of organisms, their interaction with each other, and their physical environment

famine a severe shortage of food (as through crop failure), resulting in hunger, starvation, and death

hydrophobic tending to repel, and not absorb water or become wet by water

irrigation the method of providing water to agricultural fields

La Niña periodic, significant cooling of the surface waters of the equatorial Pacific Ocean, which causes abnormal weather patterns

migration the movement of persons or animals from one country or locality to another

pollutants the foreign materials which are harmful to the environment

precipitation the falling to Earth of any form of water (rain, snow, hail, sleet, or mist)

stressors processes or events that cause stress

susceptible yielding readily to or capable of

symbiotic the interaction between organisms (especially of different species) that live together and happen to benefit from each other

vulnerable someone or something that can be easily harmed or attacked

INDEX

Photo Credits

Photographs sourced by Macaw Media, except for: Dreamstime.com: Alexugalek 16, Designua 18, Tupungato 20, Roza 24, Warren Rosenberg 25, Chuyu 37. Arnaud Bouissou/Medde/SG/COP2/Flickr 38.